THE MAGIC BED:
A BOOK OF EAST INDIAN FAIRY TALES

This edition published by Lector House in 2023

ISBN: 978-93-5800-764-0

Lector House LLP
Registered Office: H. No. 96, Block C, Tomar Colony,
Burari, Delhi – 110084, India
info@lectorhouse.com
www.lectorhouse.com

THE MAGIC BED:
A BOOK OF EAST INDIAN FAIRY TALES

HARTWELL JAMES

2023

LECTOR HOUSE LLP

The Princess Lalun

ALTEMUS' FAIRY-TALES SERIES

THE MAGIC BED

A BOOK OF EAST INDIAN FAIRY TALES

EDITED WITH AN INTRODUCTION
BY
HARTWELL JAMES

WITH FORTY ILLUSTRATIONS
BY JOHN R. NEILL

Contents

List of Illustrations

Page

INTRODUCTION

India is undoubtedly the home of the fairy-tale. Of those now in existence, probably one-third of them came from India. Gypsies, missionaries, travelers, and traders carried them to other countries where they were told and retold until much of their original form was obliterated, and many of their titles lost.

The "Jatakas," or birth-stories of Buddha, form the earliest collection of fairy-tales in the world, and were gathered together more than two thousand years before the Brothers Grimm—well and justly beloved of children—began to write the stories which have delighted a world of readers, young and old.

It is from these, and from others told by native nurses, or ayahs, to children in India--where the belief in fairies, gnomes, ogres, and monsters is still widespread--that five stories most likely to interest young people have been selected to form this volume. They are stories which have aroused the wonder and laughter of thousands of children in the far East, and can hardly fail to produce the same effect upon the children of America.

H.J.

THE MAGIC BED

THE MAGIC BED

The Ant-King extols the beauty of the Princess Lalun, the Tiger gives the Prince the best of advice, and by the aid of the Magic Bed wonderful things occur.

ONE very hot day, a young Prince, or Rajah as they are called in India, had been hunting all the morning in the jungle, and by noon had lost sight of his attendants. So he sat down under a tree to rest and to eat some cakes which his mother had given him.

When he broke the first one he found an ant in it. In the second there were two ants, in the third, three, and so on until in the sixth there were six ants and the Ant-King himself.

"I think these cakes belong to you more than they do to me," said the Prince to the Ant-King. "Take them all, for I am going to sleep."

After a while the Ant-King crawled up to the Prince's ear as he lay there dreaming, and said, "We are much obliged for the cakes and have eaten them up. What can we do for you in return?"

"I have everything I need," replied the Prince in his sleep. "I cannot spend all the money I have, I have more jewels than I can wear, and more servants than I can count, and I am tired of them all."

"You would never be tired of the Princess Lalun," replied the Ant-King. "You should seek her, for she is as lovely as the morning."

When the young Prince awoke, the ants were all gone; and he was very sorry for this, because he remembered what the Ant-King had said about the Princess Lalun.

"The only thing for me to do," he said to himself, "is to find out in what country this princess lives."

So he rode on through the jungle until sundown, and there beside a pool a tiger stood roaring.

"Are you hungry?" asked the Prince. "What is the matter?"

"A tiger stood roaring"

"I am not hungry, but I have a thorn in my foot which hurts me very much," replied the tiger.

Then the Prince jumped off his horse and looked at the tiger's foot. Then he pulled out the thorn and bound some healing leaves over the wound with a piece of cloth which he tore off his turban.

Just as he was ready to mount his horse again, a tigress came crashing through the jungle.

"How nice!" she cried. "Here is a man and we can eat him."

"No, indeed," replied her husband. "He has been very good to me. He has taken a thorn out of my foot and I am grateful to him. If he wants help at any time, we must give it to him."

"We would much better eat him," grumbled the tigress, but her husband growled so in reply that she bounded off into the deep jungle.

Then the Prince asked the tiger if he could tell him the shortest way to Princess Lalun's country, and the tiger told him it was across three ranges of hills and through seven jungles.

"But," said the tiger, "there is a fakir or holy beggar in the next jungle to this, and he has a magic bed which will carry you anywhere you wish to go. Besides this, he has a bag which will give you whatever you ask for, and a stone bowl which will fill itself with water as often as you ask it. If you can get these things you certainly can find the Princess Lalun."

"Sitting under a tree"

Then the Prince was very much pleased and set out to find the fakir. He found him sitting under a tree on the edge of the jungle, his bed on one side of him and the bag and bowl on the other side.

The fakir sat very still for a long time when he heard what the Prince wanted, and then he asked, "Why do you seek the Princess Lalun?"

"Because I want to marry her," replied the Prince very earnestly.

"Look into my eyes while I hold your hands," said the fakir, and as the Prince did so, he saw that he was one who could be trusted.

Then the fakir agreed to lend him the things and to take care of his horse until the Prince came back.

"Now lie down on the bed and wish yourself in the Princess Lalun's country," said the fakir, and, taking the bag and the stone bowl in his hands, the Prince stretched himself on the bed.

Then the Prince said, "Take me to Princess Lalun's country," and no sooner had he spoken, than off he went, over the seven jungles and over the three ranges of hills, and in less than a minute he was set down within the borders of the kingdom where the Princess Lalun lived.

The name of the Princess's father was Afzal, and he was the king or Rajah of that country. So many princes had sought his daughter in marriage that he was tired of saying "No" to them. Then he tried the plan of giving them impossible tasks to do and so getting rid of them in that way, but still they kept coming, and at last Rajah Afzal concluded to keep foreigners out of his kingdom altogether. So he issued an edict that no one was to give a night's lodging to a stranger.

"'Cannot I have supper with you?'"

So when the Prince came to an old woman's cottage and asked if he might spend the night there, she told him that the Rajah would not allow it.

"Cannot I bring my bed into your garden and sleep there?" he asked. "And cannot I have supper with you?"

"I have nothing for supper but rice," said the old woman, shaking her head. But the Prince pleaded so hard to let him come in that she consented, and he put his bag on her table.

Then he spoke to the bag. "Bag, I want something to eat!" and all at once the bag opened and there was a fine supper for two people. So the old woman ate with, the Prince. The food was delicious and was served on gold plates with gold spoons.

When they were done eating, the old woman said she would go to the well for some water.

"You need not do that," said the Prince, and then he tapped the bowl with his finger. "Bowl!" he cried, "I want water!" At once the bowl filled with water and the old woman washed the gold plates and spoons.

"If you will let me stay with you a little while," said the Prince, "you may have the plates and spoons for your own." Then he ordered the bowl to fill with water again and washed his hands in it.

"Spread it gently over the Princess"

Then the Prince said, "My bowl gives me all the water I want, and my bag gives me everything else I ask for. They belong to a holy fakir, and he might be angry if you turned his things out of the house to-night."

The old woman sat very quiet for a long time and then she said, "The anger of a Rajah is something to be dreaded, but that of a fakir might be far worse."

"Did you count them?" asked the Prince. "There are twelve gold plates and twelve gold spoons." The old woman nodded, and put them away under her bed. "You may stay," she said, "but be careful that the Rajah's soldiers do not catch you."

By this time it was night and the Prince and the old woman sat in darkness, for there was no lamp in the house. "The Rajah does not allow lamps to be used," she said. "His daughter, the Princess Lalun, sits on the roof of her palace at night and shines so that she lights up the whole country."

Just then a beautiful silver radiance filled the room, and when the Prince stepped outside he saw that the Princess was sitting on the roof of her palace. Her saree or dress was of silver gauze, and her dark hair floated almost to her feet.

"The Prince told her who he was"

She wore a band of diamonds and pearls across her head, and the light that came from her was as beautiful as that of the sun and the moon and the stars together.

"The Ant-Rajah was right," said the Prince. "Her beauty turns darkness into light, and night into day. I should never be weary of the Princess Lalun."

"The Princess sits on the roof"

At midnight the Princess came down from her roof and went to her room. Then the Prince sat down on his bed with his bag in his hand. "Bed," said he, "take me to the Princess's palace!" So the bed took him where she lay fast asleep. Then he shook the bag. "Bag," he said, "I want a lovely shawl, embroidered in red and blue and gold!" The bag gave it to him and he spread it gently over the Princess. Then the bed carried him back to the old woman's cottage.

The bag gave the Prince and the old woman breakfast and dinner and supper the next day, and when night came the Princess again sat on the roof. This time her saree was of white silk covered with diamond butterflies, and she shone more gloriously than before.

"The Rajah sent for the Prince"

At midnight the Princess went to her room again, and then the Prince told his bed to take him again to the palace. He said to his bag, "Bag, I want a very beautiful ring!" The bag gave him a ring set with rubies, which he slipped on the Princess's hand as she lay asleep, and then when she woke the Prince told her who he was.

When the Princess saw what a noble, handsome young man he was, and heard that he was the son of a great Rajah, and that he was the one who had brought her the magnificent shawl the night before, she fell in love with him and said she would tell her father and mother that she wanted him for her husband. Then the Prince went back to the old woman's cottage.

The Rajah Afzal, Princess Lalun's father, sent for the Prince the next day, and told him he might marry the Princess because she wished it.

"But first," said he, "you must do this for me. Here are eighty pounds of mustard-seed, and you must crush the oil out of them in one day."

"It is impossible," said the Prince as he went away from the palace. "How can I do it?" And when the old woman heard of it she said, "It is quite impossible. Only an army of ants could do it."

Then the Prince thought of the Ant-Rajah, and at the very minute he thought of him, the Ant-Rajah and all his ants crept under the door and into the room.

"If I do not crush all the oil out of this mustard-seed before to-morrow morning, I cannot marry the Princess Lalun," the Prince said, showing the bag to the Ant-Rajah.

"His tigers came in"

"We will attend to it for you," replied the Ant-Rajah. "Go to sleep and leave it to us." When the Prince awoke in the-morning there was not a drop of oil left in the mustard-seed, and with a light heart he took it to the King.

"That is very good, indeed," said Rajah Afzal, "but I have something else for you to do. One day when I was out in the hills I caught two demons, and I have them here shut up in a cage. I want them killed, because they may break out some day and harm my people. You may marry the Princess Lalun if you can kill them."

"How can I fight two demons?" the Prince asked the old woman when he was back in her cottage.

"Only a couple of tigers could do it," replied the old woman; and as soon as the Prince remembered his tigers they came in at the door.

"Take us to the King," said the tiger.

When the Prince asked the Rajah if the tigers might fight the two demons, he said they might do so, for he was very anxious to get rid of the demons. So all the court went to see the fight, and the tigers killed the demons.

But when the Prince said, "Now you will give me your daughter," Rajah Afzal replied, "There is only one thing more. If you can beat my kettledrum you shall marry the Princess Lalun."

"He beat the kettle-drum loudly"

"Where is your drum?" asked the Prince.

"Up there in the sky," replied the Rajah.

"I don't know how I can get up into the sky," sighed the Prince. "This is the hardest task of all." So he went back to the cottage and said to the old woman, "My ants crushed his oil, my tigers killed his demons, but who is to get up into the sky and beat his kettle-drum?"

"You are rather stupid," said the old woman. "If your bed carried you across seven jungles and over three ranges of hills, don't you think it can take you up into the sky?"

"It is very singular I never thought of that," cried the Prince, and then he sat down upon his little bed. Up into the sky it flew, where he beat the kettle-drum so loudly with the handle of his hunting-knife that the King heard him.

"The wedding shall take place as soon as you like," said the Rajah when the Prince came down again; and so the Prince sent the bed and the bowl and the bag back to the fakir.

Then invitations to the wedding were sent to all the kings and queens of the neighboring countries; and after they were married the Prince took the Princess Lalun home to his own country.

THE WISE JACKAL

"They came to a beautiful palace"

THE WISE JACKAL

Showing how the Rajah's daughters ran away from home, how they got into trouble in consequence, and how the jackal helped them.

ONCE there were two princesses whose father, the Rajah, was too busy with affairs of state to look after them. They were lonely and neglected, for they had a stepmother who treated them very cruelly. They lived in a beautiful palace, but nothing was done to make them happy or contented, for even the servants were afraid of the Rajah's second wife.

"I am going to run away," said the elder princess to her sister. "Will you go with me, Dehra!"

"Where can we go?" replied Dehra.

"There are a great many places where we can go," said Nala, "but first we will go into the jungle. We will make a little house of tree branches and have beds of grass and flowers and there will be plenty of fruit to eat."

"I will put on my blue silk saree," said Dehra, "and my pearl necklace, and you must wear your yellow silk and your rubies, and then if we meet any one they will know we are princesses."

"If we wear our jewels people may steal us," replied Nala. "We would better tie them in a corner of our sarees. We will wear our bangles, though, for all girls wear them."

The sarees that the princesses wore were long lengths of silk which they wound about their waists and then brought over their heads. They were not at all like the dresses American girls wear, but they were of beautiful material and Nala and Dehra looked very fine in them.

"'I am going to run away'"

So the little princesses went a long way into the jungle, where they found all the fruit they wished to eat, and were happier than they had been for a long time, watching the green parrots flash in and out between the trees and the monkeys chattering as they swung from bough to bough.

After a while they came to a beautiful white marble palace with a great gateway standing wide open, and over it was written in golden letters:

"Enter, Nala, do not fear;
Silver and gold await you here."

But the words changed as soon as they had read them into these:

"Follow her, Dehra; you shall see
How kind and cruel Fate can be."

The sisters looked at each other, and then Dehra said, "I do not think mine is as nice a verse as yours, Nala. It makes me feel shivery."

"It frightens me a little, too," replied Nala. "I wonder if this palace belongs to a Rakshas."

Now a Rakshas is a kind of ogre, and no one but a Rakshas would have built such a beautiful palace in the middle of a jungle.

"If it does, he may come back at any time and eat us up," said Dehra, more alarmed than ever. "Let us go away."

"The Rakshas has gone away," said a little jackal with a friendly face, who came running up to the princesses, "and you can stay in his palace for quite a while. I will let you know when he is coming back."

"They found a beautiful marble tank"

So the princesses went through the great gateway and across the courtyard into the palace, where they found gold and jewels and lovely silk dresses, and a beautiful marble tank filled with the clearest of water, where they could bathe every day.

Red lotus leaves floated on the water, and the sisters twined some of them in their hair, for the red lotus is a royal flower and princesses may wear them.

"If any stranger comes here," said Nala, "and asks for food or a drink of water, when you are alone in the house, be sure to smear your face with charcoal and put on some ragged clothes to make yourself look ugly before you let them in."

"Why must I do this?" asked Dehra.

"Because if they see how pretty you are they will take you away and we shall not see each other any more."

"You must do the same then," said Dehra, "for you are prettier than I," and then the princesses looked over the edge of the tank at their reflections in the water. Both were lovely, but Nala was a little taller than her sister and a little more graceful. Both had beautiful complexions, with teeth like pearls and eyes that shone like stars.

One day while Dehra was in the jungle talking to their friend the jackal, a prince who had been out hunting came to the palace and asked for water, as he and his attendants were very hot and thirsty. But before Nala went to see what they wanted she covered her silk dress with a ragged one and made her face dirty with charcoal.

"Nala cried out 'Oh, oh!'"

When the Prince's attendants saw a dirty-faced, ragged girl admit them to such a beautiful palace, they laughed outright, but the Prince said to himself, "If her face and hands were clean and her clothes mended, she would be a very pretty girl."

Neither Nala nor the Prince could understand each other, but at last she made out that he was thirsty, so she hastened to bring him a pitcher of water. But instead of drinking the water, the Prince threw a part of it over Nala's head and face!

Very much surprised, Nala cried out, "Oh, oh!" and started back, but the charcoal was washed from her face, and there she stood, the loveliest maiden the Prince had ever seen, even in her ragged dress, and he fell in love with her at once.

He unfastened the ragged dress and it fell off, leaving her prettier than ever in her yellow saree and a string of great rubies around her neck.

"My father is a Rajah," said the Prince, "and I am going to take you to his palace, and you shall be my wife."

Then a beautiful palanquin was brought and Nala was carefully placed in it and carried away from the Rakshas' palace. On they went through the jungle, and the frightened Princess could only pull aside the curtains and look out upon the Prince riding ahead on his white horse, while the monkeys swung from the boughs and the parrots darted in and out among the branches as they had done on the day when she and her sister had run away from their cruel stepmother.

She was very unhappy and sobbed out, "Oh, Dehra, Dehra! I want you, and what will you do without me?"

And then Nala began to think how she should let her sister know the way the Prince had taken her, so she tore a little piece off her saree and wrapped one of her rubies in it and dropped it on the ground.

She kept on doing this every little while until only one ruby was left, but they had now come to the palace of the Rajah and Ranee, the Prince's father and mother.

"Follow her, Dehra," she remembered the golden letters had said, and so Nala dropped the last of her rubies just outside the palace, saying to herself, "If Dehra does follow me, the rubies will lead her to me."

The Prince's father and mother welcomed the beautiful Princess very gladly. The Rajah gave her a new ruby necklace and the Ranee was delighted at the prospect of such a beautiful daughter-in-law. In a week they were married and every one was very kind to Nala.

But poor Dehra sat in the Rakshas' palace crying as if her heart would break. "Nala, Nala! where are you?" she cried over and over again, but no one answered her.

Then she went out of the palace, past the tank where the red lotus flowers lay on the clear water, saying to herself, "Some one has stolen her."

Then she looked at the golden letters over the gate.

"Follow her, Dehra; you shall see
How kind and cruel Fate can be."

"Half of it is surely true," she said aloud, and suddenly, from behind her, the jackal asked, "Which half is true?"

"The Rakshas is on his way home"

"Fate has not been kind yet, so it must be the last part," sobbed Dehra.

"I think that is very ungrateful of you," said the jackal. "Here you have been living comfortably in a beautiful palace for some time. I am not sure that it is nice of you to complain that you have had no luck at all."

Dehra began to cry.

"But that is not what I came to tell you," the jackal added. "The Rakshas is on his way home and you will have to go away."

He was a very wise jackal, so he went on. "It is sure to come out all right, and I will help you to find your sister."

So they went, right away, into the jungle, and pretty soon the jackal's sharp eyes saw the first ruby, wrapped in its yellow silk, lying on the grass. And soon after that they found another, and then another, and by and by they came out of the jungle.

"I shall have to leave you here," said the jackal. "There are towns out here in the open country, and where there are towns there are men, and men do not like jackals."

"But what shall I do?" asked Dehra.

"I will help you to make yourself look like an old woman," replied the jackal. "You will have to do something of the kind or some one will carry you off and you will never find your sister."

Then the jackal showed Dehra a plant which she rubbed on her face and made it an ugly brown, and then he showed her how to make her face look wrinkled. Then he went to a little house not far away and stole a coarse red saree which an old woman had hung on a bush to dry after washing it.

"Where did you get this?" asked Dehra, as the jackal brought it to her in his mouth; and the jackal told her it was growing on a bush. So Dehra put it on and went slowly along the road like an old woman.

Every little while she found one of Nala's rubies, and then they would be a long way apart, but at last she came to the city where Nala was, and found the last ruby by the gate of the Rajah's palace. Then she sat down not very far away and wondered how she could get inside the palace.

As night came on, the wife of a laboring man took pity on the poor old woman, as she supposed Dehra to be, and let her sleep in a hut in her garden. Now this garden was very near the palace grounds, in which was a marble bathing-tank covered with red lotus flowers.

"Twined red lotus flowers in her hair"

When Dehra saw this beautiful place, she said to herself, "I will bathe there every morning. I will go very early, so as not to be seen."

So Dehra left her hut very early and bathed in the beautiful tank, and all the brown stain and all the wrinkles came off her face. She washed the old saree and hung it on a tree, and then put on her own blue silk saree and her necklace of pearls. Then she sat on the steps of the tank and twined some of the red lotus flowers in her hair.

"It makes me feel like myself again," she thought, as she looked down at her reflection in the water. But the royal lotus flowers made her think of Nala, and she longed more than ever to see her.

After Dehra had bathed in the palace gardens for several mornings, his servants told the Rajah that some of his beautiful lotus flowers disappeared each day before sunrise. This made the Rajah very angry and he said he would offer a reward for the capture of this thief.

Then the Rajah's second son, who was a very handsome young prince, said to his father, "You need not do that. I will capture the thief without any reward."

"He will do it easily," said the Ranee, who was very proud of her son.

So that night the Prince walked about the palace garden for a long time, but at last he was so sleepy that he lay down near the bathing-place and did not awake until the sun was just rising.

Leaning against the steps of the marble tank was a lovely girl dressed in blue silk with a chain of pearls around her neck and red lotus flowers in her hair.

The Prince jumped up quickly, exclaiming, "You cannot be the thief!"

"I did not mean to be a thief," faltered Dehra.

"They are my father's flowers and you can have more of them if you wish," said the Prince without taking his eyes off her lovely face.

"Oh, no!" said Dehra, running to get the old red cotton saree. "Please do not tell any one you have seen me."

"You must have come from Nala's country," replied the Prince, "for you talk as she does."

The old woman's dress dropped from Dehra's hands.

"Is Nala here, and do you talk to her?" she asked. It had been so long since she had heard her sister's name spoken that it seemed like listening to sweet music.

"Indeed, Nala is here," said the Prince. "She is my brother's wife and we all love her. She is so beautiful that she is called the 'Star of the Palace,' but you are prettier than she is."

At these words all Dehra's fear left her, and when the Prince said, "Let us go and find Nala," she let him take her hand and lead her into the palace, where every one said, "She is exactly like our young Rajah's wife!"

"'They are my father's flowers'"

Then the Prince led Dehra into the presence of the Rajah and Ranee, and there she told them that she was Nala's sister and how she had come a long, weary way in search of her. Then the Prince asked permission to marry Dehra, and his father and mother were so pleased with the beautiful girl that they said he might do so as soon as he liked.

Then Dehra was taken to a beautiful room, hung with silk curtains and lighted by jewelled lamps. Nala was dressed in the richest silks and jewels, as the wife of a young Rajah should be, but there was a look of sadness on her beautiful face, for she was thinking of the sister from whom she had been separated so long.

"Oh, Dehra!" she said, as she looked up and saw her sister standing before her. "Oh, Dehra! Fate has been kind at last." And then the sisters kissed each other again and again, and when Nala heard that Dehra was to marry her husband's brother and all live together in the palace, she could hardly believe that it was true.

Then Dehra said, "The jackal told me that everything would come out right in the end, and so it has."

"He is a nice jackal," replied Nala. "The golden letters over the gateway to the Rakshas' palace ought to be changed to:

'Seek long, seek far, and you shall find
To patient seekers Fate is kind'

and if he were here I would ask him to have it done."

THE FOUR BROTHERS

"A diamond shining in his forehead"

THE FOUR BROTHERS

Relating how a baby with a diamond in his forehead grew to be a man, and what he did for his brothers.

IN the very heart of the jungle there stood a very old tree. It was older than any other tree there and had seen many wonderful things. It was very wise, too, and knew many secrets.

Every spring it put out fresh green leaves and lovely white blossoms, but one year the flowers were more beautiful than ever, and among them, on one of the lower branches, was a bud which hung there like a silver globe among the green leaves.

"I wonder why that bud is so much larger than the others," said the rose-apple tree, who had a great deal of curiosity.

"It holds a secret," replied the fig-tree, who was quite a gossip and loved to talk to the other trees.

"But when shall we know the secret?" asked the rose-apple tree.

"In the middle of the night there will be a thunder-storm and then the bud will open. You will see it by the lightning."

But when the storm came and the thunder roared and the lightning flashed, the rose-apple tree was afraid and dared not look up. But the fig-tree watched the grand old tree stretch its branches out bravely to the tempest, and in the midst of it saw the white bud burst open as the third bough laid it gently on the ground.

Inside the flower lay the prettiest little baby ever seen, curled up as if asleep, as lovely as a flower himself, and then his eyes opened and he lay smiling at the sky and watching the blue-white lightning flashing across it.

Then when morning came and all around was bright and calm and still once more, the baby put out his tiny hand and played with the flowers.

"He must be a wonderful baby," said the fig-tree. "See his little white silk shirt; it is just the color of the flower in which he was born, and look, he has a diamond shining in his forehead!"

"Perhaps it is a star and not a diamond," said the rose-apple tree; but because of its brightness it could not tell which it was.

Then the humming-birds and the parrots and the monkeys and the jackals all came to look at the baby. "He would be better off if he had wings like mine," said a humming-bird.

"Or if he had plumage like mine," said a parrot.

"Fur like mine would be much better for him," added a jackal; but they all agreed that he was a very wonderful baby, or he would not have a star in his forehead.

By and by the child cried just a little bit, for he was hungry, but the fig-tree bent a bough and dropped honey into his mouth, and then he smiled again.

And then when sunset came a tigress stole quietly up to the child.

"I'll bring my cubs here," she said to herself. "He will do for their supper." But the flowers and the grasses covered him up so that she could not find him when she came back again.

"We will not let any harm come to him," said the flowers and the grasses. "He is our baby."

"What shall we call him?" asked the trees, and the old tree which had borne the beautiful bud said, "His name is Nazim, and you must all of you take care of him and teach him the secrets of the jungle."

And so as Nazim grew up, the trees and the wild flowers and all the creatures in the jungle taught him all they knew. The monkeys taught him how to climb trees, and Dame, the great turtle who lived in the river, taught him how to swim.

The humming-birds showed him where the wild fruits grew and which of the blossoms had honey in their cups; and he learned to know the herbs which would heal bruises, and how to charm the jungle snakes, and many other things which children who live in houses never know.

Early every morning he bathed in the river, hanging his white silk shirt to dry on a tree, and at night he slept in a hammock under the fig-tree, which the flowers made for him of their twining tendrils.

"The monkeys taught him to climb trees"

He became a tall and beautiful boy, as good and gentle as he was strong and fearless, and as for clothes, his white silk shirt grew as he grew and never wore out or wanted mending. All the animals in the jungle loved him, even the tigress who had wanted her cubs to eat him when he was a baby.

One day Nazim said to the old tree, "There are a great many parrots and jackals and monkeys. Are there no others like me; is there only one Nazim?"

And the old tree asked, "Why do you want to know?" And Nazim replied wistfully, "I should like to see them."

Then the old tree said, "Climb to my topmost branch, and tell me what you see;" and when Nazim had done this he cried out, "I see a hill with a very sharp point."

"Near the top of that hill, which is the needle-shaped hill, is a tree covered with bright pink blossoms. It is called Kidsadita," said the old tree. "Go up to it and smell the flowers and ask where the Four Brothers are."

So through the jungle Nazim ran to the needle-shaped hill, and there was Kidsadita, the pink-flowering tree. "Where are the Four Brothers?" he asked, as he smelt the blossoms.

"All the animals loved him"

"On the other side of the hill," said Kidsadita. "They are preparing their supper."

Then Nazim went on, around the hill, and there were four tall men cutting up a deer which they had killed. As he came near they thought they had never seen so beautiful a boy, and ran to meet him. He was indeed a beautiful boy, dressed all in white, the star shining in his forehead and a look of gentle love on his face.

"We are four brothers; will you be the fifth?" they asked Nazim. "Will you be one of us?"

"I will be your brother," replied Nazim, "for that is why I came. All the creatures in the jungle had brothers and sisters, and I had none. I wanted to find some brethren."

Then Chimo, the youngest brother, said there were two things they wanted. One of these was fire to cook their meat, for they were obliged to eat the flesh of the deer raw; and the other was a wife for each of them.

Then one of the other brothers said that the giant Rikal Gouree had a fire burning on his hearth and four daughters who were anxious to get married. They knew that he lived not very far away, but they had never been able to find his house, so they were still without wives and firebrands to light the wood with which to cook the deer they killed.

"Four men cutting up a deer"

"If you will give me a bulrush," said Nazim, "I will show you the way to his house." So Chimo brought him a bulrush and Nazim fitted it to his bowstring; then he bent the bow, letting the bulrush fly straight to Rikal Gouree's palace. "Follow my arrow," cried Nazim. "It has cleared a path for you, and you shall find what you want."

Then the Four Brothers followed the path Nazim's arrow had made, but Chimo, who was the swiftest runner, came to the giant's palace first.

Rikal Gouree was sleeping by the fire in an immense room where the couches were twenty feet long and eight feet high. The fireplace was like a huge, red, glowing cavern in which whole tree-trunks lay burning instead of logs, and the ceiling was so high that Chimo could hardly see it.

Chimo stole a look at the sleeping giant and then snatched up a firebrand and ran for the door. But as he passed the sleeping giant a spark from the brand lighted on Rikal Gouree's hand.

The giant sprang up with a cry of pain and rushed out of the house after Chimo, but could not catch him. In his flight Chimo dropped the fire-brand and got back to his brothers with nothing to show for his trouble but a bad fright.

"We want to leave Rikal Gouree alone," he told them. "I would rather eat raw flesh all my life than go near that monster again."

"Chimo dropped the firebrand"

Finding he could not catch Chimo, the giant went back to his house and into the room where his wife and four daughters were. He was very cross, for he had lost his nap and the burn on his hand pained him.

As soon as he had thrown himself into his great chair his oldest daughter asked him, "Have you got husbands for us yet?" Every day one of his daughters asked him this question and the sulky old giant would reply, "No! who can get husbands for four daughters all at once?"

Then the youngest daughter asked her father who the young man was that she had seen running away from the house. He told her that while he was asleep a young man had come in and stolen a firebrand.

"I think you did very wrong to send him away," said the giant's wife. "He would have been one husband at any rate, and giants' daughters do not get husbands easily. Here is the arrow which came into the room this morning, which was a sign that men would soon follow it. You have done a very foolish thing and we shall probably suffer for it."

Some giants' wives are afraid of their husbands, but this one was not, and she went on to give her husband such a scolding that Rikal Gouree was glad to get away and go to sleep by the fire again.

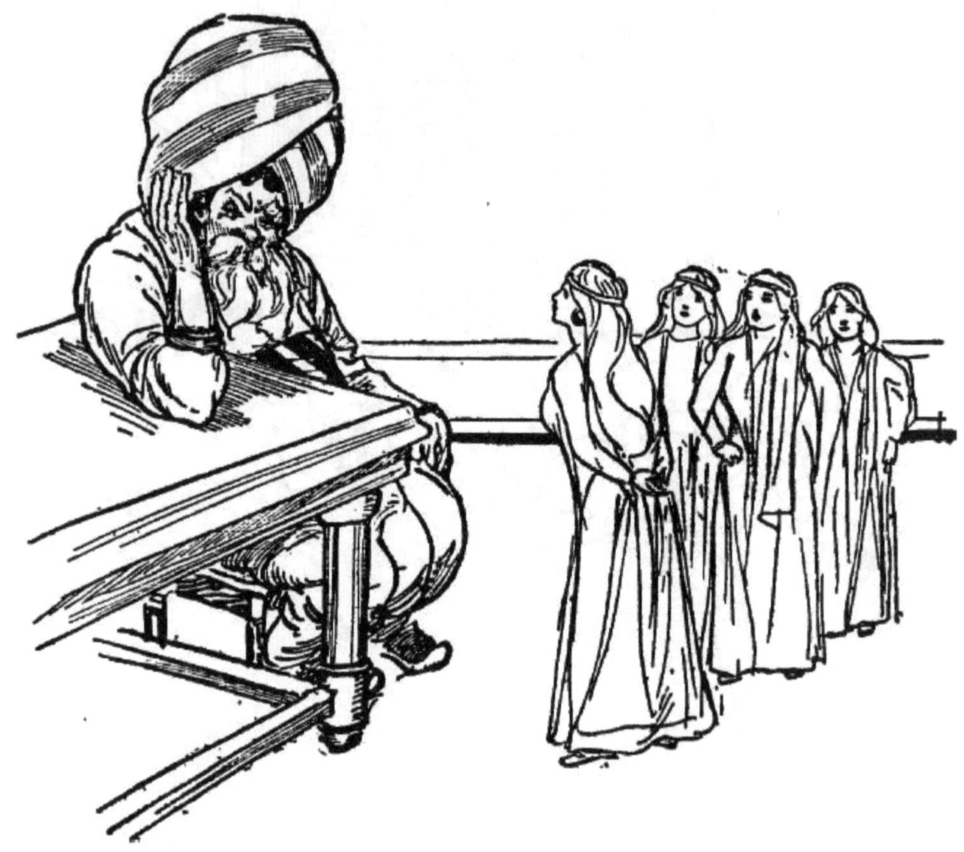

"'Have you got husbands for us?'"

After a while the giant was awakened by beautiful music which came from a tree which grew close to his palace wall. He lay still enjoying the sweet sounds, but presently they seemed to call him outside, and looking up he saw Nazim sitting on one of the branches of the tree playing on a lute.

Underneath the tree the dogs and cats and all the other animals belonging to him were listening to the music, and the boughs were covered with birds who were listening too. Presently the music grew so merry that Rikal Gouree held up his skirts and began to dance.

"What a silly old man you are!" cried his wife as she came out of the house and saw what he was doing. "You silly old man!" But in a few minutes she was dancing too, holding up her saree with one hand like a young girl, while her bangles and anklets tinkled merrily.

Then the giant called to Nazim, "Here, young man, come down from the tree and I will give you anything you want."

"Then you must give me your four daughters," said Nazim. "Each of my four brothers wants a wife, and you must give us, besides, a firebrand from your hearth."

"I knew the arrow was a true omen," cried the giant's wife, and then his daughters came forward and gave Nazim his arrow, which they had kept very carefully. They were so pleased that they said good-bye to their father and mother, and taking as many clothes and jewels as they could carry on their heads, they set out with Nazim.

"Their clothes on their heads"

On they went until they came to the needle-shaped hill where the pink-flowering tree Kidsadita was, and there they married the Four Brothers and lived very happily together.

Nazim did not want to marry, and because he was better and wiser than they, the Four Brothers made him their king. The giant's daughters made their jewels into a crown for him, but no jewel was as bright as the star in his forehead, which outshone them all.

THE FISH PRINCE

"'You have broken my enchantment'"

THE FISH PRINCE

A Prince is changed into a fish by his cruel mother. The enchantment is broken by the aid of a seven-headed cobra, and all ends well.

ONCE there were a king and queen who had two sons. The older of the two was a very short and ugly man with only one eye, and that was in the middle of his forehead. His brother was tall and handsome and carried himself like a prince.

Naturally the king preferred his handsome son and wished to make him his heir. "My people will never obey a dwarf with only one eye," he said.

This made Deesa, the older son, very angry. "The kingdom ought to be mine," he said, "or if I cannot have it all it should be divided."

He said this to his wife, whose name was Matni, and as she was an enchantress she determined to get the whole of the kingdom for her husband if possible. She thought it all over and then invited the younger brother to a banquet in that part of the palace where she lived.

Then she said to her husband, "After supper you must sit with your brother on the balcony overlooking the river. I will change him into a fish and then you can throw him into the water. In this way we shall hear no more of him."

"'The kingdom ought to be mine'"

"Threw some powder on his head"

Deesa agreed to this, and after supper invited his brother to sit with him on the balcony. Then Matni went up on the roof of the palace and threw down some powder on the younger Prince's head. Just as soon as she did this, the Prince was changed into a little fish, and his brother picked him up and threw him into the river.

All this was done so suddenly that the Prince hardly knew what had happened to him. Over and over he turned before he struck the water, but when it had closed over him he found that he had been changed into a fish and could swim very nicely underneath the water.

"He was caught in a net"

He seemed to know, too, that Matni had enchanted him, and he wanted to get out of her way; so he swam on and on until at the end of two days he was outside of his father's kingdom.

Then one day he was caught in a net by some fishermen and taken to the palace of the king of that country to be served up for dinner. He was not very big, and one of the servants thought it would be much nicer to have him in a bowl than to cook him.

"The Queen became fond of him"

So the servant begged for the little fish. "I will take it to the Queen's room," she said. "She has no children and is sometimes very dull. This little fish may amuse her."

The Queen was very much pleased with the pretty little fish and became very fond of him. When he grew to be too large for the bowl, she had another one prepared for him, and fed him boiled rice twice every day. "He is such a dear," she said, "that he shall be called Athon-Rajah, the Fish Prince."

After awhile the Fish Prince grew so big that the Queen had a tank made for him through which the clear water of the river flowed in and out.

Then one day the Queen feared that the Fish Prince was not comfortable in his tank and would prefer to be in the beautiful shining river which flowed past her windows. So she said to him one day, "Are you quite happy here, Athon-Rajah?"

After a moment's thought the Fish Prince replied, "I am quite happy here, dear Queen-mother, but if you could get me a nice little wife I should be happier. It is really quite lonely here all by myself."

Now the Queen looked upon the Fish Prince as her own son, and never imagined that any girl would have the least objection to marrying him. So she said, "If you want a wife I can easily find one for you."

"'I will find you a wife at once'"

"But would you not like to go and swim in the river?" she went on.

"Certainly not," replied the Fish Prince. "All I want is to have a nice little wife and live right here." The answer astonished the Queen, but then she did not know that he was a fish only in appearance.

"All right," she said. "I will find you a wife at once, and have a room built in the tank for her." She had the room built at once, but it was not an easy matter to find a wife for the Fish Prince!

Everybody knew that Athon-Rajah was a pet of the Queen's, but for all that, they said he was a monster of a fish, and that all he wanted of a wife was to devour her. But the Queen sent messengers far and wide, among the rich and the poor alike, but found no one who was willing to give his daughter as a wife to the Fish Prince.

Even the people who had eight or ten daughters were very polite about it, but said, "We cannot give one of our children to your Fish Prince." Then the Queen offered a great bag of gold to any father who would send his daughter to be the Fish Prince's wife, but nothing came of it for a long time.

At last a fakir or beggar-man heard of the bag of gold and said to the messenger, "You may have my eldest daughter. She cannot be worse off than where she is now, and the gold will make me rich."

"Tell me where she is?" asked the Queen's messenger.

"She is down by the river, washing," said the man. "She is my first wife's child, and her stepmother makes her do all the hard work, and will not give her enough to eat."

"'You can take her and welcome'"

"She gets more than she deserves," cried the stepmother angrily. "Much more than she deserves. You can take her and welcome. We shall be well rid of her, and if the Fish Prince wants to eat her, he can do so."

"The cobra put out his seven heads"

So the messenger gave the bag of gold to the fakir, and went down to the river, where he found a very pretty girl washing clothes on the edge of the water. She cried very much when she heard what his errand was, and begged him to let her say good-bye to an old friend before he took her away.

"'I want to see my wife!'"

"Tell me who is this friend," said the messenger. "The Queen said we were to lose no time." And the girl replied, "It is a seven-headed cobra whom I have known ever since I was a little child."

Still crying, the girl, whose name was Maya, ran along the bank, and the cobra put his seven heads out of the hole where he lived.

"I know all about it," he said. "Don't cry. Pick up those three pebbles outside my hole and put them in your dress. When you see the Athon-Rajah coming, throw the first at him. If it hits him he will sink to the bottom of the tank."

Then the cobra went on. "When he rises to the surface, hit him with the second, and the same thing will happen. Throw the third pebble at him, and he will change from a fish into a handsome young prince."

"Then he isn't really a fish?" asked Maya.

"He is the son of a Rajah and is under an enchantment," replied the cobra. "But you can break the enchantment in the way I have told you."

So Maya dried her tears and went away with the messenger to the palace, where they showed her a beautiful little room that had been prepared for her inside the tank where the Fish Prince lived. Then the Queen kissed her and said, "You are just the dear little wife I want for my Athon-Rajah."

Maya would have been quite happy, for every one was very kind to her, if it had not been for the thought of the cold dark water, and her fear that she might not be able to hit the Fish Prince with the pebbles. But she let them put her into the little room, where she sat down and waited for a long time, with the pebbles in her hand.

"Changed into a handsome prince"

Then there was a sound of rushing water and of waves dashing against the door. She looked out and there was a huge fish swimming towards her with his mouth wide open!

"I want to see my wife!" cried the Fish Prince. "Unfasten the door!"

Trembling from head to foot with fright, Maya opened the door and threw the first pebble, which went right down his throat. He sunk like a stone, but in a minute or two came up to the surface again.

Then Maya threw the second pebble, which hit the Fish Prince on the head, and he sunk the second time.

Maya was so nervous that she nearly missed hitting him with the third pebble, for it only touched the tip of his fin. This time he did not sink, but changed into a handsome prince, who took her in his arms and kissed her tenderly.

"You have broken my enchantment!" he cried. "Now we can enjoy sunshine and happiness in the world above, and need not live in a tank any longer."

So they were drawn up out of the water and taken to the palace, where no one could possibly live happier than Maya and the Fish Prince.

THE TALKING TURTLE

"'Two wild ducks are carrying a turtle!'"

THE TALKING TURTLE

Relates the unique and satisfactory end of a turtle who made mischief among the cranes, fishes, parrots and monkeys. The moral is obvious.

A GREAT many years ago there was a king who talked too much. His name was Badahur, and from his beautiful palace he ruled many millions of people.

There was also a turtle who was even fonder of talking than the King, and he lived in a pond in the King's garden.

But for all the King was so great and so rich, his people did not respect him because he talked and talked about everything under the sun. He had a sort of prime-minister whose name was Hazar, and he was expected to say foolish things, of course, but the King seemed to want to say them all.

When the King drove through the streets in his golden chariot with footmen running before and behind, even the beggars by the roadside would say, "There goes one who cannot hold his tongue."

"Don't tell your secrets to Badahur," they would go on. "He says more foolish things in a day than Hazar will ever say in his life. He talks and talks, and no one else has a chance to speak where he is."

All this used to trouble Hazar, for he knew what the people thought of their king. He used to lie awake at night thinking how he could cure the King of his talkativeness, but he could settle upon no plan, for the more he thought the more difficult the matter seemed.

But the turtle was even worse than the King in the matter of talking. He talked to the fishes, the parrots, the monkeys, and the birds all day long, until they were tired of the very sound of his voice.

"'Tells the cranes where our hiding-places are'"

The fishes, as they lay under the bank used to say to each other, "He is a mischief-maker. He tells the cranes where our hiding-places are, and then they drag us out with their long bills and eat us."

He told Mirbah, the King-parrot, what the monkeys said about his tail, and that started such a quarrel between the parrots and the monkeys that it never will be patched up.

"When the King takes the court away to the summer palace, let us hope that some one will invite the turtle to make a long visit elsewhere," said the humming-birds. "He is a horrid gossip, even worse than Hazar."

By and by the hot days came and the King and his court went to their beautiful summer palace away up on the slopes of the mountains. No one asked the turtle to go anywhere and he was left in the pond.

One day Hazar, who had stayed in the city to finish up some business before joining the King, was walking in the garden near the pond and saw two wild ducks alight on the ground near where the turtle was basking in the sun.

As soon as the turtle saw the ducks he began to talk to them. "Where are you going?" he asked.

"There is a place called the Golden Cave up in the mountains where we used to live, and we are going back there," replied the wild ducks.

"I should think that would be a very nice place," said the turtle. "Is there a pond in the Golden Cave?"

"'Where are you going?' he asked"

"No. But we have lakes and rivers, plenty of them, and they are very much better than such a pond as you have here. If you will come with us you can see for yourself."

Something of this kind was just what the turtle wished, for he was tired of living in the pond in the King's garden. His tongue had made him so many enemies that things were unpleasant for him there.

"But I do not see how I can go with you to the Golden Cave," he said to the wild ducks. "If I could fly it would be an easy thing to do."

"If you would like to go, we will take you," said the ducks. "We will take the two ends of a stick in our bills, and you can hold on to the middle by your mouth. Just don't let go of it, and you will be all right."

"Oh, that will be easy for me to do," replied the turtle.

"Indeed it won't," said Hazar to himself from behind the trees, where he was watching the ducks and the turtle; "you would have to hold your tongue, and that is something you could never do since you were born."

Hazar finished up the business he had on hand and then joined the King in his summer palace up in the hills and as soon as they found a stick which would bear the weight of the turtle, the ducks flew up into the air with the turtle between them.

How the fishes did laugh as they looked at the turtle hanging from the stick by his mouth. "Don't come back again, Talking Turtle," they called after him. "We can get along very well without you."

"Hanging from the stick by his mouth"

"I don't intend to come back! Keep your old pond to yourselves!" was what the turtle wanted to say in reply, but he did not dare to, because if he opened his mouth to speak he would tumble right back into the pond again.

So they flew on and on over the cities and villages and fields, and every time they stopped, the ducks cautioned the turtle to hold his tongue or he would be killed.

Then one day as they were flying over a field, a woman who was working there called out, "Two wild ducks are carrying a turtle along on a stick!"

This made the turtle so angry that he wanted to say, "You miserable woman, what is it to you?" but he controlled himself, although he bit the stick half way through in his rage.

After a while the ducks and the turtle came to the mountains and flew directly over King Badahur's summer palace. Some boys in the town below threw sticks at the ducks and called out to them, "Drop that fat old turtle. We'll make soup of him!"

This made the turtle so angry that he could no longer keep silence. He started to say, "Soup! You shall be made into soup yourselves, miserable children," but as he opened his mouth to utter the first word, he let go of the stick and crashed down into the courtyard of the palace, where the King and a number of his courtiers were walking. Hazar ran to pick him up, but he was quite dead!

"Hazar ran to pick him up"

"What do you think of this?" asked the King of Hazar. "Did the turtle drop from the sky as a warning to us?"

"He was being carried through the air by two wild ducks," replied Hazar. "With your Majesty's permission I will tell you what I know about him." And then he told the King what he had heard and seen in the palace garden.

After Hazar had finished his story, the King was silent for a long time and then he said, "This disaster happened to the turtle because he could not hold his tongue."

Hazar bowed and the King was silent again. "It strikes me, Hazar," he said at last, "that at times I talk too much."

"A golden turtle was set up in the palace"

All the courtiers looked at Hazar, expecting him to deny that the King could talk too much, or to say that it was a pleasure to listen to anything the King had to say, but Hazar did nothing of the kind. He quietly said, as he looked the King straight in the face, "Happy is the kingdom where the king knows his own faults!"

"Happy is the king who has such a faithful counsellor as yourself, Hazar," responded the King. "To remind us of the fate of this turtle, we will have a golden one set up in the palace."

So a golden turtle was made and set up in one of the great halls of the palace, and whenever the King saw it he was reminded of the fate of the talkative turtle. He learned wisdom and discretion and how to keep silent when it was necessary, and instead of despising him, his subjects came to love and respect him.

Printed by Libri Plureos GmbH in Hamburg,
Germany